The Journey to Financial Freedom

THE JOURNEY TO FINANCIAL FREEDOM

Six Basic Facts About Financial Empowerment

By

JOHN KENNEDY AKOTIA

The Journey to Financial Freedom

Copyright © 2014 JOHN KENNEDY AKOTIA

All rights reserved. No part of this publication may be used or reproduced in any form or by any means, or stored in a data base or retrieval system, or transmitted in any form or by any means without prior written permission, except in the case of brief quotations embodied in critical articles and reviews.

ISBN-13: 978-1502897763

Request for information should be addressed to
The Administrator
Destiny Impact Publications
P. O. Box BG 106
Bolgatanga, UER, Ghana, W/A

Mobile: +233 50 2538473
Email: fitzjkenny@yahoo.co.uk

The Journey to Financial Freedom

TABLE OF CONTENTS

Introduction……………………………………………………..4

Dissatisfaction With Your Present Financial State………8

Desire For Change……………………………………..30

Decision To Take Personal Responsibility……………….46

Determination To Follow Through With The Decision…66

Duty To Act On Your Decision……………..…………….81

Diligence To The Actions Of Your Decision…………..125

Introduction:

What Is Financial Freedom?

Financial freedom refers to a state of financial self-sufficiency, which enables a person to have more than enough for him or herself and to take care of other people's needs as well. It also means having more than enough financial resources for the present and for the future.

Financial freedom enables you to live your life in such a way that you do not spend most of your life working for money but rather, money working for you.

Financial freedom is an essential and an integral part of the Christian faith. Jesus had financial sufficiency, if not; he would not have employed a financial manager and treasurer in the person of Judas Iscariot.

God does not only endorse financial freedom for His children, He actually empowers them and teaches them as well to prosper.

Deut. 8:18

*But **thou shalt remember the Lord thy God: for it is he that giveth thee power to get wealth**, that he may establish his covenant which he sware unto thy fathers, as it is this day.*

Isaiah 48:17

*Thus saith the Lord, thy Redeemer, the Holy One of Israel; **I am the Lord thy God which teacheth thee to profit**, which **leadeth thee by the way that thou shouldest go.***

In this book, *"Journey to Financial Freedom"* we are going to be considering some basic truths about financial empowerment, which are as follows:

Dissatisfaction with your present state
Desire for change
Decision to take personal responsibility
Determination to follow through with the decision

Duty to act on your decision
Diligence to the actions of your decision
Luke 15:11-20

And he said, A certain man had two sons: [12] And the younger of them said to his father, Father, give me the portion of goods that falleth to me. And he divided unto them his living. [13] And not many days after the younger son gathered all together, and took his journey into a far country, and there wasted his substance with riotous living. [14] And when he had spent all, there arose a mighty famine in that land; and he began to be in want. [15] And he went and joined himself to a citizen of that country; and he sent him into his fields to feed swine. [16] And he would fain have filled his belly with the husks that the swine did eat: and no man gave unto him. [17] And when he came to himself, he said, How many hired servants of my father's have bread enough and to spare, and I perish with hunger! [18] I will arise and go to my father, and will say unto him, Father, I have sinned against heaven, and before thee, [19] And am no more worthy to be called thy son: make me as one of thy hired servants. [20] And he arose, and came to his father. But when he was yet a great way off, his father saw him, and had compassion, and ran, and fell on his neck, and kissed him.

1

Dissatisfaction With Your Present Financial State

The journey to financial freedom begins with dissatisfaction with your present financial state. Until you are discontent with where you are currently there is no way you are going to desire a new state or change. Change is a product of the dissatisfaction of a present state of affairs.

If the financial state you find yourself in at the moment is not a source of worry to you, you will never see the need to want something different. Until you become uncomfortable with something, you will never see the need for an alternative. As long as you can make do with your present situation and you do not have any serious reservations, nothing in you will ever prompt or challenge you to look at any other thing.

Many of the people who walk about in life without purpose and without dreams only end up with mediocre attainments. This is because, they never dreamed beyond where their eyes could see. They never had any aspirations for great accomplishments because, they never saw anything wrong with their current state of affairs anyway and so there was no way they could think of accomplishing anything more.

You can easily resign your life to fate and end up in total defeat should you find yourself in a state of despondency and not know what to do with your life in the midst of your predicament. If on the other hand you find yourself in a state of life you are not satisfied with and that dissatisfaction can generate enough positive anger in your heart, not for people but for the situation you find yourself in, there will always be created in you a desire to want to see a change.

Necessity they say is the mother of invention and productivity, but until that necessity generates holy passion to want to see a change it cannot mother any act of invention or productivity in your life. This is because, inventions and improved productivity are birthed from the wombs of intensive dissatisfaction with current state of affairs and levels of attainment. This then leads to the desire to want to see something new.

The prodigal son became dissatisfied with the despondent state he found himself in. In life, until you become passionately angry with any state or condition you find yourself in and become dissatisfied enough, you will probably remain in that state or condition. The process of dissatisfaction that led to the desire to see a change in the life of the Prodigal son who is our case study in this book metamorphosed through the following eight conditions as enumerated in Luke 15: 14 - 17.

Luke 15:14-17

14 And <u>when he had spent all</u>, <u>there arose a mighty famine in that land</u>; and <u>he began to be in want</u>.

15 And <u>he went and joined himself to a citizen of that country</u>; and <u>he sent him into his fields to feed swine</u>.

16 And <u>he would fain have filled his belly with the husks that the swine did eat</u>: and <u>no man gave unto him</u>.

17 And when <u>he came to himself</u>, he said, How many hired servants of my father's have bread enough and to spare, and I perish with hunger!

a) When He Had Spent All

Luke 15:13
And not many days after the younger son gathered all together, and took his journey into a far country, and there wasted his substance with riotous living.

Money is a proud goddess that shies away from those who abuse her and treat her with contempt. When you violate the cardinal law of wealth generation that says "money attracts money", money will forever avoid you in life. But if you respect money and appreciate the law of "money attracting money", you continually attract money into your life from unexpected sources.

Money has no racial or tribal inclinations. It is however, governed by strict principles and laws that are both spiritual and physical. There is an interesting biblical account of a parable in which talents (different amounts of money) were given to certain individuals for a period of time after which time they were called to account for the monies that were given to them to keep till their master returned from the journey he was embarking upon.

In that scripture, the first two servants brought back their monies they have doubled through various investments. The third servant however, brought back the same amount of money the master gave him, which he apparently buried in the ground and upon the return of the master he went and dug the money and brought it back with no interest or profit earned on it. Jesus commanded that they take the pound from the unprofitable servant and give it to the servant that already had ten pounds.

The people around Jesus being ignorant of this law of money immediately reacted by calling Jesus' attention to the fact that, that man already had enough money to deserve that additional money whiles they didn't have anything. Jesus on the contrary reminded them of this law of money thereby even giving it a spiritual backing.

For I say unto you, ***That unto every one which hath shall be given****; and from him that hath not, even that he hath shall be taken away* *from him.*

When we get money and violate this law of "money attracting money", we would finish spending the money and there will not be any income producing opportunity provided for us. The prodigal son went away to blow his portion of the inheritance he received forcefully from the father.

"And not many days after the younger son gathered all together, and took his journey into a far country, and there wasted his substance with riotous living".

This is the financial state of many of us. We tend to blow every penny we ever earn the moment we earned it and wait for the next pay cheque to come our way, whether by chance or by choice. You cannot continue to live your life as a spendthrift and expect to attain financial independence anytime soon because; financial profligacy is a sure recipe for personal financial bankruptcy.

The prodigal son is described as wasting his substance with riotous living. Riotous living refers to a lifestyle devoid of restriction and characterised by lack of discretion. He went on drinking sprees, definitely coupled with womanizing and its associated vices. He definitely had hordes of fellow young men and women the money attracted to him who helped him squander his inherited wealth with the wanton and unruly behaviour. Because, the Bible says in Ecclesiastes 5:11 that:

When goods increase, they are increased that eat them: *and what good is there to the owners thereof, saving the beholding of them with their eyes?*

If you want to become financially empowered, don't walk in the footprints of this young man. You must learn to spend your money with discretion, so that you don't learn the lesson he learned the way he did. So we have learnt that the Prodigal son's journey to the dissatisfaction of his current state began with him having exhausted his substance with riotous living.

b) There Arose a Mighty Famine in That Land

Anytime we foolishly squander our wealth or substance in such an unruly manner, the next possible thing that confronts us is shortage. Most often after we have experienced seasons of personal financial boons comes seasons of shortage such that if we did not make provision for such seasons of shortage we are found wanting. This was the case of this young man. After he had finished squandering his substance there arose a mighty famine in the country he went to sojourn in to squander his wealth.

*And when he had spent all, **<u>there arose a mighty famine in that land</u>**; and he began to* *be in want.*

Life is full of cycles of favourable and unfavourable seasons succeeding each other. Anytime you are experiencing a favourable season in life and you fail to recognise the fact that an unfavourable season could come after that season of abundance you will surely be caught up in the same predicament as the Prodigal son.

In order to become financially empowered, you must learn to take charge of your finances in such a way that you will be able to make provision for your unfavourable financial seasons during the favourable seasons when you command abundance. The Bible teaches of the wisdom of the ant in the book of Proverbs 6:6-8

6 Go to the ant, thou sluggard; consider her ways, and be wise:
7 Which having no guide, overseer, or ruler,

8 Provideth her meat in the summer, and gathereth her food in the harvest.

The ant is a very small insect among the creatures on earth yet it is full of wisdom. The wisest king that ever lived - King Solomon - studied the life and ways of several creatures of God that epitomize wisdom and found the ant to be one of such creatures that exhibit such wisdom as is needful for life on earth. He chose therefore to admonish the sluggard to go to the ant and consider her ways and be wise. One interesting characteristic feature worthy noting about the ants is that they have no guide, overseer, or ruler that gives them instruction as to what to do at what time, yet by their own volition or instinct know what they are supposed to do and they do exactly that.

The ants are able to tell the seasons and thus prepare appropriately for each season. They know the difference between summer and winter and that summer precedes winter. They therefore use the summer season to gather all the food they would need for fall and winter when the climatic conditions will become too harsh to support life outside their holes.

To become financially empowered, you should be able to tell the difference between financial summer and winter. You must understand the dynamics of money and wealth creation in that there is a season for money when you can gather it and there also comes a season that you can no longer gather any more of it.

Prov. 27:23
¶ Be thou diligent to know the state of thy flocks, and look well to thy herds.
24 For riches are not for ever: and doth the crown endure to every generation?

c) He Began To Be In Want

In the midst of the mighty famine that came upon the land, the young man began to be in want because he had squandered all his substance and did not make any provisions for the future. Many of us fail to "make hay whilst the sun is shining" and therefore have no provender when the rains set in.

In the study of personal finance, you might have come across the term "rainy day". This does not refer to a physical rain that would be falling. It is a term used to describe the fact that in your financial dealings, you must be prudent enough to put money aside in savings for any unforeseen eventualities of life.

Life is full of uncertainties and the bad news is that these uncertainties don't pre-inform you before they come. Most certainly too, they come in a way that you may not have enough time to now want to run around to mobilize the necessary financial support to respond to them.

This was the predicament of the Prodigal son. He did not anticipate this evil that came upon him suddenly and since he was not prepared for it, it took him by storm and he began to be in want.

d) He Went and Joined Himself to A Citizen of That Country

When you are in want and desperately need help, you can resort to do anything for survival, irrespective of how demeaning or dehumanizing it may be. When the famine came upon the land and the prodigal son began to be in want, his next line of action was to find a rescuer in order to put soul and body together to survive. He had no friend or family to turn to in that land. Nobody was ready to receive him in to their home in the most difficult time of his life. Even the people who helped him squander his wealth all deserted him to fulfil the scripture that says:

Prov. 19:4, 7
4 ¶ Wealth maketh many friends; but the poor is separated from his neighbour.

7 All the brethren of the poor do hate him: how much more do his friends go far from him? he pursueth them with words, yet they are wanting to him.

He finally decided to join himself to one of the citizens of that country to do any menial job he could, just to get food to eat. There are many people in this life that are in that state right now. They are supposed to be princes and royals by birth but are turned into hired servants and labourers of the basest depravity. Not because they were destined to be so but because, of the choices they make and courses of action they take in life.

Any man that seeks early gratification in life is not a likely candidate for financial freedom. Because the Bible says in Proverbs 20:21 that "An inheritance may be gotten hastily at the beginning; but the end thereof shall not be blessed." Don't be in a haste to attain financial gratification in life but rather seek to build enough wealth to last many days and possibly to outlive you so that there can be an inheritance for your children after you.

Prov. 24:27
Prepare thy work without, and make it fit for thyself in the field; and afterwards build thine house.

If you will consider the above scripture, you can do yourself a lot of good when it comes to the subject of financial freedom and seeking early gratification. The verse says you must take time prepare your work, build your investment and financial base and make it fit, strong, solid, consistent and guaranteed for you in the field before you think of building your house. Gratification should therefore be at the tail end of a solid financial system that guarantees you long lasting financial future.

Advice is cheap but actions are costly. Take counsel and be wise so that you do not find yourself in the predicament of the young man whose life we are looking at. May you not get to the place in your life when you will need to join yourself to any man for a menial job you were not originally created or destined to do. You were destined to be great and wealthy and you can't settle for anything less than that.

e) He Sent Him into His Fields to Feed Swine

The prodigal son upon his new appointment became a caretaker of swine thus turning a prince into a companion of pigs. Anytime you abuse royal position and opportunities, you are most likely to fall from glory to grass. The prodigal son, from the position of throwing expensive and irresponsible parties for friends and funs all too soon is now in the position of throwing food to pigs.

Anytime your position and status in life changes, your association also changes in sync with your new position and status. When the status of the young man changed from **rich man** to **poor man**, immediately, his company changed from friends and funs to swine. This, as we have mentioned earlier on is in fulfilment of scripture that says wealth makes many friends; but the poor is separated from his neighbours and all the brethren of the poor do hate him and his friends go far from him and that even though he pursues them with words, yet they run further away from him. When this happens to you, the only option left for association is to be friends with things that are indifferent as to whether you are rich or poor, and pigs became his new friends, neighbours and brethren.

f) He Would Fain Have Filled His Belly with the Husks That the Swine Did Eat

Associating with swine though dehumanizing is not as bad as settling to **dine with pigs**. The passage said "he would <u>fain</u> have filled his belly with the husks that the swine did eat". The word 'fain' used here is an archaic word, which means: to be well-pleased, glad, satisfied, content or delighted. Let us see how the above line would read if we replace the word 'fain' with its modern variants so we can appreciate the full import of the despondent state the young man found himself in.

"He would **have been well-pleased, glad, satisfied, content, and delighted to** have filled his belly with the husks that the swine did eat"

By the time a man gets to this state, then it means things have really gone bad and absolutely out of hands. Dining with pigs would have been a welcomed miracle to this young man but even that did not materialise as we would soon read in the next point

g) No Man Gave Unto Him

There can be nothing as devastating in life

as to be rejected by friends and people that contributed to your downfall or current state and then be denied even the basest form of a dehumanizing privilege such as desiring to eat food served to swine. This however, was the point the prodigal son got to in his life. The passage we have been looking at so far says "He would have been well-pleased, glad, satisfied, content, and delighted to have filled his belly with the husks that the swine did eat: and **_no man gave unto him_**."

The rejection of friends, neighbours and funs though painful was overlooked and life continued. The desire to have filled his belly with the husks that the swine did eat though dehumanizing was endured. Nevertheless, the denial of even the basest form of a dehumanizing privilege such as desiring to eat food served to swine was the last straw to break the camel's back and that brought this young man to the turning point of his life, the dissatisfaction with current state of affairs.

h) When He Came To Himself

As indicated above, you could bear the rejection of friends, neighbours and funs though painful, and still let life continue. You could also somehow develop the inner strength to endure the shame of having to settle for husks that swine did eat as your food though degrading. Nonetheless, to be refused or denied even this base form of a dehumanizing privilege should break down the strongest ego and wake one up to the reality of humility.

*And when **he came to himself**, he said, How many hired servants of my father's have bread enough and to spare, and I perish with hunger!*

Every one of us at one point in time in our lives comes to terms with the reality of this verse and have to swallow our pride, break the back of our ego, humble ourselves and brace up for the reality of life.

The verse says when 'he came to himself'. You must come to your senses, which is the breaking point of dissatisfaction that gives birth to the desire for change. The young man, I believe sat down and reflected on life until the scales fell of his eyes and he realized that even swine at this point in time had greater value than him. Then the thought of being a hired servant in his father's house dawned on him.

You must be dissatisfied enough to desire a change in life, and until you get here in your life, financial freedom would only be a mere "nine days' wonder" to you for the rest of your life. Come with me as we explore the next basic fact on our journey to financial freedom, which is "Desire for Change."

2

Desire For Change

Once you become dissatisfied with your present state, a desire for change will automatically be birthed in your spirit. I said desire not a wish. A wish is mere fantasy of an ideal state of life but backed with no decision to attain it. A desire on the other hand is a strong longing, craving, yearning or aspiration for something, which is backed by decision or action to achieve it.

Desire is the starting point of all achievement and the first stage of riches. Every form of wealth accumulation and journey to financial freedom must begin with a state of mind called burning desire. Wishing for financial freedom does not bring you financial freedom, but desire that is backed by a purposefulness of mind and a determination to follow through with your decision to attain financial freedom will surely land you in your financial freedom.

Passion is an essential ingredient on the journey to financial freedom. However, passion is birthed in the cradle of desire. When you have desire for something and fan that desire ablaze into a burning desire until it becomes an obsession, it produces passion.

Desire does not call for special abilities or education. It does not take special effort to develop desire for wealth. If only you can get to the point where you become unhappy with any current state of affair you find yourself in and see the possibility of change with your mind's eye, you will immediately develop a craving for that change and that is the birth of desire. If you become unhappy with the kind of food you eat, a desire for change would be birthed. If you become dissatisfied with the kind of house you live in and the suburb of the city you find yourself in, desire for change would be birthed. So, like we have discussed earlier, desire for change is rooted in the dissatisfaction with a present state which you can no longer tolerate or cope with.

The prodigal son, after becoming dissatisfied with the despondent state in which he found himself, started desiring for a change in his situation.

And when he came to himself, he said, How many hired servants of my father's have bread enough and to spare, and I perish with hunger!

Prosperity cannot be dumped on any man. Neither does any man stumble into wealth that leads to financial freedom. You can never expect to have anything you do not have a burning desire for. You cannot become successful in life if you do not at some point in your life desire to be successful in life. Desire is the prerequisite even for answered prayer because, the Bible says in Mark 11:24 that

*Therefore I say unto you, What things soever ye **desire**, when ye pray, believe that ye receive them, and ye shall have them.*

Our prayer requests made to God must begin with a desire for the things we are requesting Him to do for us. The scriptures also tell us that if we are willing and obedient, we shall eat the good of the land. It is not obedience alone that is required for us to qualify to eat the good of the land but our willingness to want to enjoy the good of the land. It means you can be obedient alright, but until you show your willingness to want to receive the good things of the land, you are not going to receive.

Likewise, if you don't desire a change or quest for financial prosperity and financial freedom you cannot possibly attain financial freedom.

Prov. 13:12, 19

12 ¶ Hope deferred maketh the heart sick: but **when the desire cometh, it is a tree of life.**

19 ¶ **The desire accomplished** is sweet to the soul: *but it is abomination to fools to depart from evil.*

The Keys to Developing Desire for Change:

There are keys to developing the desire for change on the journey to our financial Promised Land. Among these keys are the following five as we discuss in the next few pages as we conclude this chapter on desire for change.

a) The first key is a sudden awakening to the fact that the state or condition you find

yourself in is too appalling to be your portion in life.

Living in a hopeless financial state can be likened to being in a state of drunken stupor. Until you decide to wake up from that state to face the reality of life, your condition will continue to be miserable. You can never desire a change of condition until you wake up to the fact that the state or condition you find yourself in is too appalling to be your portion in life.

The prodigal son for some time resigned his life to fate, threw in the towel and accepted the financial condition he found himself in as his portion in life. But upon second thought, he decided to reanalyse the situation more carefully and at this time refused to accept that despondent state as his portion in life. It was there and then the passage says when he came to himself; he said, how many hired servants of my father have bread enough to eat and to spare, and I perish with hunger!

b) The second key is when your mind's eye begins to see alternatives that are better than your despondent condition.

This second key to developing a desire for change is the ability to see or picture alternatives that are better than your current hopeless condition. This follows the principle of self-attainment that says that

"anything you can visualise, you can develop the willpower to attain it."

The power of visualisation is therefore an essential ingredient to developing the desire for change on our journey to financial self-sufficiency or freedom. The power of visualisation is what God used to train the Patriarch, Abraham's mind to believe God for his own biological seed and spiritual descendant after him and also to receive by faith the lands of the heathen nations God promised to give to Abraham's descendants.

Gen. 15:4-6

4 And, behold, the word of the LORD came unto him, saying, This shall not be thine heir; but he that shall come forth out of thine own bowels shall be thine heir.

5 And he brought him forth abroad, and said, **Look now toward heaven, and tell the stars, if thou be able to number them: and he said unto him, So shall thy seed be.**

6 And he believed in the LORD; and he counted it to him for righteousness.

Gen. 13:14

14 ¶ And the LORD said unto Abram, after that Lot was separated from him, **Lift up now thine eyes, and look from the place where thou art** *northward, and southward, and eastward, and westward:*

15 **For all the land which thou seest, to thee will I give it,** *and to thy seed for ever.*

16 And **I will make thy seed as the dust of the earth: so that if a man can number** *the dust of the earth, then shall thy seed also be numbered.*

17 Arise, walk through the land in the length of it and in the breadth of it; for I will give it unto thee.

The law of visualisation is a very powerful tool for attaining financial freedom because, before you physically attain any level of financial success you must be able to visualise that success first before it materialises. This is the law that propelled the prodigal son into the realisation that though he had squandered his legitimate portion of the family inheritance, he still stands some chance because, he visualised how hired servants in his father's house had the luxury of enough food to eat and even spare some.

If only you can visualise where you want to be or could be financially, irrespective of your current situation or condition, you could generate enough desire for change to propel you out of that current unpalatable financial state.

The key however, is that the law of visualisation must be at work; that is, the ability of your mind's eye to begin to see and visualise alternatives that are better than your current despondent condition.

c) The third key is when you can envisage possible opportunities that are available to you for your change.

Another key to developing desire for change is the ability to spot opportunities that are available to you for your change. Until you can envisage what chances or opportunities are available to you for a possible change it will be difficult for you to desire a change in the first place. Your ability to discover these opportunities will give you a glimpse of hope that all is not lost and that there is still a ray of light at the end of the tunnel.

Every misfortune in life carries with it a proportionate amount of fortune. The only difficulty is the ability of the individual involved to do due diligence to spot this hidden fortune. The prodigal son was smart enough to do exactly that and that showed him the ray of light at the end of the tunnel that sparked hope in him to desire a change of his condition. The young man thought within himself and concluded that even if he could not be accepted back as a son, at least he could apply for a job as a hired servant and that he convinced himself he would not be denied.

Luke 15:19
And am no more worthy to be called thy son: ***make me as one of thy hired servants.***

Many of us are at that despicable place in life not because there are no opportunities for us to shift camp to where we ought to be. The truth is that we simply fail to spot the opportunities for alternatives that do exist for us to stage a comeback at life, so we are not able to develop the desire for the necessary change.

d) The forth keys is that you must be able to see the possibility for change in order to develop desire for change

The next key to developing desire for change is being able to see the possibility for change in order to develop desire for that change. The big question you should seek to find answers to anytime you find yourself in any state of financial insufficiency is: Is there room for change? Are there possibilities for change in this situation? Can things change for the better?

The definite answer is a big YES! Because we say no condition is permanent. Since change itself is the only constant in life, it means every other condition, situation, circumstance, or state of affairs could be changed if the appropriate steps are taken to that effect. The prodigal son saw the possibility of a change in his financial predicament. He saw the possibility of being accepted back as a son on the ground of mercy and sympathy or in a worst case scenario, being engaged as a hired servant. So to him there was the possibility of acceptance which provoked the desire for change in him.

e) The fifth key is the ability to brace yourself up to face any possible opposition that may confront you in case you decide to go for a change.

The final key to developing the desire for change for our discussion is most probably the greatest stopper of many would be candidates of financial self-sufficiency from staging a comeback at life after they have taken an initial beating from life. There are people who when they fail in life once, would never recover from the temporary failure to stage a comeback. Success in life, in any field of endeavour is not about never failing in life. Success is your ability to get up and get going after a temporary failure. The road to financial freedom can be rough some times and you would have to take quite a number of beatings from life before getting to your financial destination. It therefore requires some amount of resilience and persistence.

In order, therefore to be able to develop the desire for change, you have to brace up to face any possible opposition that may confront you in case you decide to go for a change. The prodigal son though optimistic that the outcome would be good should he return home and plead for clemency. Nevertheless, I believe, he braced himself up to face any possible opposition that may confront him. For example, had his elder brother instead of staging a peaceful protest to the father decided to go hostile against him, may be the story would have been different.

A typical example in the Bible, of a man that returned home for reconciliation and prepared for the odds, was Jacob when he returned from his uncle Laban's house and Esau came to meet him. Even though Jacob was optimistic and anticipated a peaceful reconciliation with the elder brother whom he offended before leaving, he all the same did not throw caution to the wind, in the event that things turn out the other way round. So he devised a strategy of dividing his company in to separate groups so that all of them did not come face to face with Esau at the same time. This implied that Jacob braced himself up to face any possible opposition that may confront him and his entourage.

If you have courage enough to brace up to face any possible opposition that may confront you in case you decide to go for a change, you will be on your way to developing a desire for change in your pursuit of financial freedom.

We have been discussing in this chapter the fact that you need to develop the desire for change as a key to attaining financial freedom and having done that, you will need to decide to take personal responsibility for your financial condition at present and where you want to get to next. Come with me then to the next chapter where we discuss the decision to take personal responsibility for your financial self-sufficiency.

3

Decision To Take Personal Responsibility

> *You must take personal responsibility. You cannot change the circumstances, the seasons, or the wind, but you can change yourself.*
>
> **JIM ROHN**
> (America's foremost business philosopher)

Everywhere you look, even in these economic times of uncertainty, growing numbers of people are feasting on incredible banquets of prosperity, while most of the rest settle for the crumbs that fall from the table.

The journey to financial freedom starts the moment you decide that you were destined for prosperity, and not for scarcity; for abundance, and not lack. Is there not a part of you that has always known this? Can you for once in your lifetime see yourself living a bounteous life - a life of "more than enough"? It only takes a moment to decide; so why not decide right now that you are destined for prosperity and not scarcity and so you are making up your mind to embark on the journey to financial freedom. If you can reach that decision right now, then it means you are ready to accept personal responsibility to take your financial destiny into your own hands and then begin to walk on your own financial highway.

A Decision is a choice or resolve to do something. Every serious desire must be followed by this resolve called decision

Taking Charge of Your Financial Destiny

The Law of Financial Independence states that:

> "The starting point for achieving financial independence and becoming a self-made millionaire is for you to accept complete responsibility for your financial life."

Many people never do this. They instead go through their days, and their financial life, trusting to luck, with the idea that somehow, someday, someone else will come to their rescue.

The average financial freedom seeker today believe they are entitled to a great life but somehow, somewhere, someone (certainly not they themselves) is responsible for filling their lives with continual happiness, exciting career options, nurturing family time, blissful personal relationships and financial sufficiency, simply because they exist.

Nevertheless, the hard truth and the one

lesson this chapter in particular and may be this whole book is based on is that there is only one person responsible for the quality of the life you live and your financial freedom. And that person is you!

If you want to be successful, you have to take 100% responsibility for everything that you experience in your life. This includes the level of your achievements, the results you produce, the quality of your relationships, the state of your health and physical fitness, your income, your debts, your feelings and everything!

This is not easy.

In fact, most of us have been conditioned to blame something outside of ourselves for the parts of our life we don't like. We blame our parents, our bosses, our friends, our co-workers, our spouse, the weather, the economy, the government, our astrological chart, our lack of money - anyone or anything we can pin the blame on. We never want to look at where the real problem is, which is, ourselves.

There is a wonderful story told about a man who was out walking one night and came upon another man down on his knees looking for something under a streetlight. The passer-by inquired as to what the other man was looking for. He answers that he was looking for his lost key. The passer-by offered to help, got down on his knees, and helped him search for the key. After an hour or so of fruitless searching, he said, "We've looked everywhere for the key and we haven't found it. Are you sure that you lost it here?"

The other man replied, "No, I lost it in my house, but there is more light out here under the streetlight."

It is time to stop looking outside yourself for the answers to why you haven't created the life and results you want, for it is you who creates the quality of the life you lead and the results you produce. It is you and no one else!

To achieve major success in life you must assume 100% responsibility for your life.

Taking 100% responsibility means you acknowledge that you create everything that happens to you. It means you understand that you are the cause of all of your experiences. If you want to be really successful, and I know you do, then you will have to give up blaming and complaining and take total responsibility for your life. That means all your results, both your successes and your failures. That is the prerequisite for creating a life of success. It is only by acknowledging that you have created everything up until now that you can take charge of creating the future you want.

This thought of the prodigal son about his condition brought him to his senses and he realized his end if he continued thus. He compared his lot with that of the hired servants of his father, and thus making his final decision to go back home and plead for the lowest position in the household.

Luke 15:17-19
*[17] And when he came to himself, he said, How many hired servants of my father's have bread enough and to spare, and I perish with hunger! [18] **I will arise and go to my father**, and **I will say unto him**, Father, **I have sinned against heaven**, and before thee, [19] And **I am no more worthy to be called thy son**: make me as one of thy hired servants.*

Financial freedom thus requires a decision to take personal responsibility to effect a change in our financial state. Because, to be truly rich and financially independent, you must believe that it is your personal responsibility to create your own financial life instead of believing that it will just happen to you.

If you want to create wealth, it is imperative

that you believe that you are at the helm of affairs in your life, especially your financial life. If you do not believe this, then you must inherently believe that you have little or no control over your life, and therefore you have little or no control over your financial success. You have to believe that you are the one who creates your own success just as you are the one who creates your mediocrity. More so, that you are the one creating your struggle around money and success, whether consciously or unconsciously, it is still you.

Instead of taking responsibility for what is going on in their lives, many people embarking on the journey to financial freedom rather choose to play the role of the victim. A victim's predominant thought is often "poor me." So presto, by virtue of the law of intention, that is literally, what victims get: they get to be "poor."

Notice that we did not say they are victims, but we said they play the *role* of victim. I do not believe anyone is a victim in life. I believe people play the victim because they think it gets them something. We will discuss this in more detail shortly.

It is possible to tell when people are playing the victim in their pursuit of financial freedom. They tend to show all or some of the following attitudinal traits: They play the blame game, they justify their situation and they are always complaining.

a) **They Play the Blame Game**

At the heart of the reason, why most people are not rich is the *"blame game syndrome."* Most victims are professionals at the "blame game." The object of this game is to see how many people and circumstances you can point the finger at without ever looking at yourself. It is fun, at least for the person playing the victim. Unfortunately, though, it is not such a fun for anyone else who is unlucky enough to be around him or her. That is because; those in close proximity to victims become easy targets of their blame game.

These people with the victim mentality tend to blame the economy or the government. If they happen to be investors, they would blame the stock market and blame their broker. If they were entrepreneurs, they would blame their type of business. If they are employees, they would blame their employer, they would blame their other colleague employees; they would blame their manager and even blame the head office. If they were family people, they would blame their partner, they would blame their spouse and of course, they always blame their parents and other family relations. They have the effrontery to sometime blame even God himself. It is always someone else or something else that is to blame. The problem is anything or anyone but them.

b) **They Justify their Situation**

If victims are not blaming, you will often

find them justifying or rationalizing their situation by saying something like "Money's not really important." Wait a minute! Let me ask you this question: If you said that your husband or your wife, or your boyfriend or your girlfriend, or your partner or your friend, were not very important, would any of them be around for long? I do not think so, and neither would money!

Would you have a new car if it were not important to you? Of course, you will not. Would you have a pet dog if it were not important to you? Of course, you will not. In the same way, if you do not think money is important, you simply would not have any of it.

Imagine you are in a conversation with a friend who tells you, "Money's not important or money isn't everything." Put your hand on your forehead and look up as though you are getting a message from the heavens, then exclaim, "You are broke!" To which your shocked friend will undoubtedly respond, "How did you know?"

To put it bluntly: no one who says money is not important has any! Rich people understand the importance of money and the place it has in our society. On the other hand, poor people validate their financial ineptitude by using irrelevant comparisons. They will argue, "Well, money isn't as important as love." Now, is that comparison dumb or what? What is more important, your arm or your leg? Maybe they are *both* important.

Listen up, my friends: Money is extremely important in the areas in which it works, and extremely unimportant in the areas in which it does not. Moreover, although love may make the world go round, it sure does not pay for the building of any hospitals, churches, or homes. It also does not feed anybody.

Money is therefore extremely important in the areas in which it works, and extremely unimportant in the areas in which

it does not.

If you are still not convinced, try paying your bills with love. Or else try paying for your gas at the gas filling station after you have bought gas for your car. No rich people believe money is not important. In addition, if I have failed to persuade you and you still somehow believe that money is not important, then I have only two words for you, *you're broke,* and you always will be until you eradicate that non-supportive file from your financial blueprint.

c) They Are Always Complaining

Complaining is the absolute worst possible thing you could do for either your health or your wealth. This is because of the belief in the universal law that states, "What you focus on expands." When you are complaining, what are you focusing on? Is it what is right with your life or what is wrong with it? Chances are you are obviously focusing on what is wrong with it, and since what you focus on expands, you will keep getting more of what is wrong.

Many teachers in the personal development field talk about the Law of Attraction. This Law of Attraction states that; *"like attracts like,"* meaning that when you are complaining, you are actually attracting the very negative situations you are complaining about into your life.

You will ever notice that complainers usually have a tough life. It seems that everything that could go wrong does go wrong for them. Now that you know better what complaining can do to its victims, you can now be in a better position to explain to them why their life is crappy.

This brings us to another point. You have to make sure not to put yourself in the proximity of complainers. If you absolutely have to be nearby, make sure you bring a steel umbrella or else the crap meant for them will get you too!

Try to stay as far away from complainers as possible because negative energy can be infectious. Many people however, love to hang out and listen to complainers. Do you know why? It is simple: they are waiting for their own turn! If you have been a complainer, forget about attracting success for now; for most people, just getting to "neutral" would be a great start!

Blame, justification, and complaining are like pills. They are nothing more than stress reducers are. They alleviate the stress of failure. Think about it. If a person was not failing in some way, shape, or form, would he or she need to blame, justify, or complain? The obvious answer is no.

From now on, as you hear yourself disastrously blaming, justifying, or complaining, cease and desist immediately. Remind yourself that you are creating your life and that at every moment you will be attracting either success or crap into your life. It is imperative you choose your thoughts and words wisely!

Now you are ready to hear one of the greatest secrets in the world. Are you ready? Read this carefully: *There is no such thing as a rich victim!* Did you get that? I will say it again: There is no such thing as a rich victim.

Meanwhile, being a victim definitely has its rewards. What do people get out of being a victim? The answer is *attention.* Is attention important? You bet it is. In some form or another it is what almost everyone lives for. Moreover, the reason people live for attention is that they have made a critical mistake. Virtually all of us have made the same error. We have confused attention with love.

Believe you me; it is virtually impossible to be truly happy and successful when you are constantly yearning for attention. Because, if it is attention you want, you are at the mercy of others. You usually end as a "people pleaser" begging for approval. Attention seeking is also a problem because people tend to do stupid things to get it. It is imperative to "unhook" attention and love, for a number of reasons.

First, you will be more successful; second, you will be happier; and third, you can find "true" love in your life. For the most part, when people confuse love and attention, they do not love each other in the true spiritual sense of the word. They love each other largely from the place of their own ego, as in "I love what you do for me." Therefore, the relationship is really about the individual, and not about the other person or at least the both of you.

By disconnecting attention from love, you will be freed up to love another for who they *are,* rather than what they do for you.

Now, as I said, there is no such thing as a rich victim. So to stay a victim, attention seekers make sure they never get rich.

It is time to decide. You can be a victim *or* you can be rich, but you cannot be both. Listen up! Every time, and I mean *every* time, you blame, justify, or complain, you are *slitting the throat of your financial destiny.* Sure, it would be nice to use a kinder and gentler metaphor, but forget it. I am not interested in this kind or gentle descriptive right now. I am interested in helping you see exactly what you are doing to yourself! Later, once you get rich, we can use kinder and gentler terms.

It is time to take back your power and acknowledge that you create everything that is in your life and everything that is not in it. Realize that you create your wealth, your non-wealth, and every level in between.

You Have To Give Up All Your Excuses

Ninety-nine percent of all failures come from people who have a habit of making excuses.

GEORGE WASHINGTON CARVER
(Chemist who discovered over 325 uses for the peanut)

If you want to create the life of your dreams, then you are going to have to take 100% responsibility for your life as well. That means giving up all your excuses, all your victim stories, all the reasons why you can't and why you haven't up until now, and all your blaming of outside circumstances. You have to give them all up forever.

You have to take the position that you have always had the power to make it different, to get it right, and to produce the desired result. For whatever reason; ignorance, lack of awareness, fear, needing to be right, the need to feel safe, you chose not to exercise that power. Who knows why? It does not matter. The past is the past. All that matters now is that from this point forward you choose to act as if you are 100% responsible for everything that does or does not happen to you.

If something doesn't turn out as planned, you will ask yourself;

How did I create that?
What was I thinking?
What were my beliefs?
What did I say or not say?
What did I do or not do to create that result?
How did I get the other person to act that way?
What do I need to do differently next time to get the result I want?

4

Determination To Follow Through With The Decision

Reaching a decision to do something in life is very critical to success. However, success in any field of endeavour is contingent upon the actions taken in relation to the decisions we reach. Nevertheless, between our decision making time and the action taking time lie the most crucial defining moment as to whether our decisions will be followed through with the required actions needed for success or not.

This is where determination is required for us to be able to follow through with our decisions. For a decision to become a reality therefore, it must be backed by the determination to follow through with it.

Determination here refers to willpower, strength of mind, resolve, fortitude, purposefulness, and resilience.

The prodigal son, after reaching the decision to take personal responsibility, was so determined that, he decided he would do everything possible to return to the father and win acceptance even if it will mean losing his son-ship with the father and be considered as a servant of the father.

Luke 15:18, 19
*[18] **I will arise and go to my father, and will say unto him**, Father, I have sinned against heaven, and before thee, [19] And **am no more worthy to be called thy son: make me as one of thy hired servants**.*

Many of us make resolutions in life but are never determined enough to follow through with them, so we never get those resolutions fulfilled. Why are you giving up so soon in life?

It is because you lack the will power.

Many people set off in life on the journey to success yet when they meet with a little adversity, a little opposition, the least resistance and least failure, they give up. You will never achieve anything substantial with such an attitude but rather end up as a casualty on the journey to financial freedom. This therefore means that a decision to take personal responsibility of your financial destiny by itself is not strong enough. The decision will therefore need determination to back it up. Determination thus becomes the pushing force.

You will meet with temporary failure but you do not have to give up that easily in the face of failure. You would be faced with opposition but here again, you must learn not to give up in the face of opposition. You must be determined enough to persist in the face of adversity. You will need mental fortitude to break through the barricades of opposition, resistance and temporary failure on the way to success in any area of your life. This is because some failures in life are actually successes in disguise so you must learn not to give up in the face of temporary failures.

One of the sources of joy on the journey to success is when you go pass resistance and see the light at the end of the tunnel. Every resistance, temporary failure, opposition or challenge you are able to either surmount or circumvent becomes a reference point to get you to the next level of life.

David the shepherd boy had to relate his experience of killing both the bear and the lion with his bare hands to the task of facing Goliath the giant warrior on the battlefield. Determination therefore is the watchword here because, it is the instrument that breaks the back of resistance in order to keep you going when others are giving up.

Keys to Cultivating and Developing the Spirit of Determination

Determination can be cultivated or developed; however, this would require the use of certain turnkey principles among which are the following:

1. You must be firm in your purpose
2. Resolve not to give up too easily
3. Develop a solid mental fortitude
4. Desire to defy the odds
5. Desire to go the extra mile

1. You Must Be Firm In Your Purpose

The first turnkey principle for cultivating and developing the attitude of determination is the firmness of your purpose or your resolve.

Men of great successes in life never compromise their purpose and resolve to do the things they have been called to do. They are very firm when it comes to pursuing their purpose, and nothing dares stand in their way. Your purpose in life determines your resolve whilst your resolve births your passion.

When you allow your passion to drive you toward achieving that ultimate purpose of your life, your efforts will become unflinching. Firmness of purpose is therefore at the cradle of cultivating the spirit of determination. How firm are you in the pursuit of that single, most important purpose in your life? How resolved are you such that you will never give up in the face of adversity? How strong is your passion toward achieving that purpose? Your sincerest answers to these questions is a sure-fire proof of whether you have what it takes to cultivate and develop the spirit of determination that is strong enough to back your decision to take personal responsibility for your financial destiny

2. You Must Resolve Not To Give Up Too Easily

Another turnkey principle for cultivating and developing the spirit of determination is the resolve not to give up too easily in the face of challenges in life. The road to success is littered with countless numbers of failure stories of people who gave up either too easily or too early to the jeopardy of their dream of attaining financial success in life.

If you want to become a celebrated success story in life, then you will need as a matter of necessity to resolve not to give up too easily. Learn never to accept no for an answer until it becomes imperatively obvious that there can be nothing but no for an answer to your situation. Do not accept no for an answer when you have not explored all opportunities and alternative opportunities available.

There is this age long adage that says that "where there is a will, there will always be a way". I also want to add an improved version that says, "When there is will power, there will always be determination." Persistence therefore becomes the watchword here. If at first you do not succeed, try again and one day you will surely succeed if you do not give up.

The Journey to Financial Freedom

Read the following excerpt from the life of a man who never gave up.

"At the age of seven, a young boy and his family were forced out of their home. The boy had to work to support his family. At the age of nine, his mother passed away. When he grew up, the young man was keen to go to law school, but had no education.

At 22, he lost his job as a store clerk. At 23, he ran for state legislature and lost. The same year, he went into business. It failed, leaving him with a debt that took him 17 years to repay. At 27, he had a nervous breakdown. Two years later, he tried for the post of speaker in his state legislature. He lost. At 31, he was defeated in his attempt to become an elector. By 35, he had been defeated twice while running for Congress. Finally, he did manage to secure a brief term in Congress, but at 39 he lost his re-election bid.

At 41, his four-year-old son died. At 42, he was rejected as a prospective land officer. At 45, he ran for the Senate and lost. Two years later, he lost the vice presidential nomination. At 49, he ran for Senate and lost again.

At 51, he was elected the President of the United States of America.

The man in question: **Abraham Lincoln.**"

Author Unknown

Many of us are acquainted with this eloquent example of persistence and determination in achieving victory. We read it, stop for a moment, then sigh, and say: "Wow! That's the stuff real achievers are made off."

In saying this, it is all too easy for us to think about achievers like Lincoln almost as **"mythological creatures"**, separate from the rest of humanity and empowered with some mysterious qualities that smoothens their path towards inevitable success. This is the view of self-achievement and financial success that many people have traditionally taken: "That achievers are marked out for achievement from early on in their lives, and that if you are not an achiever; there is little you can do to become one". This should not be the case because, through patience, persistence and hard work, anyone can become a highly effective and successful achiever.

3. You Must Develop A Solid Mental Fortitude

The human mind is one of the greatest assets for achieving success in life. Your mental processes can either be your aide or adversary on the journey to success in any endeavour of life, depending on your success orientation vis-à-vis mental disposition. You will need a solid mental fortitude to cultivate and develop the spirit of determination you need to back your decision to take personal responsibility for your financial destiny.

Mental fortitude is a collection of attributes that allow a person to persevere through difficult circumstances (such as setbacks and adversities of life) and emerge without losing confidence. We can use the term liberally to refer to any set of positive attributes that help a person to cope with difficult situations. Its qualities include sacrifice and self-denial. Most importantly however, it is combined with a perfectly disciplined will that refuses to give in. It is a state of mind –you could call it 'character in action.' -

Developing mental strength is about finding the courage to live according to your values and being bold enough to create your own definition of success. Mental strength involves more than just willpower; it requires hard work and commitment. It is about establishing healthy habits and choosing to devote your time and energy to self-improvement. Although it is easier to feel mentally strong when life seems simple — often, true mental strength becomes most apparent in the midst of tragedy. Choosing to develop skills that increase your mental strength is the best way to prepare for life's inevitable obstacles.

4. Desire To Defy The Negative Odds

Another turnkey principle for cultivating and developing the spirit of determination is the desire to defy the negative odds you will encounter on your journey to financial freedom. Odds refer to the chance or likelihood of something happening. The odds are the probabilities and uncertainties of life.

On life's journeys, you are bound to encounter both anticipated and unanticipated outcomes. The question however, is "what do you do when you meet with unanticipated outcomes that are contrary to what you were expecting?" It is these anticipated and unanticipated outcomes, which are contrary to what you were expecting that I refer to as the negative odds.

The secret to cultivating the spirit of determination is to programme your internal environment to defy any such negative odds.

You are bound to meet a number of them in your life's pursuits and you must not allow them to change the course of your life. As many as may be avoidable try to avoid them but as many as are unavoidable try to defy them and keep going at your dreams and ambitions. This is because, when the going gets tough in life, it is only the tough who keep going. Toughen yourself therefore to be able to defy the negative odds lest they stop you in your success tracks.

5. Desire To Go The Extra Mile

The final turnkey principle for cultivating and developing the spirit of determination is the desire to go the extra mile. If you mean to excel in life, you must become someone who will not give up too easily. You must have the resilience of someone who runs in the marathon. If you have the stamina and mind-set of one who runs a sprint race and go to participate in a marathon, you will burn out in no time. The sprinter's eyes are usually set on the finishing line from take-off to finish because the finishing line is within view from the starting line.

This however, is not the case in a marathon race because, in a marathon race, you could not possibly view the finishing line, which is twenty-six miles away from where you are starting the race from. Your focus therefore is the next mile, then another mile, then another, until the finishing line finally comes in view before you tend to possibly sprint toward it.

You may lose count on the miles you have made and the miles ahead of you in the process so your only motivation is the resilience to make an extra mile, then another extra mile. If your mind is made like that, you will not be overwhelmed by any additional mile you did not anticipate is still ahead of you. This is because, all throughout the race, you have programmed your mind to go the next extra mile.

Life is not a sprint race but a marathon, which requires a lot of stamina and resilience to bounce back each time you fall on the way. You will definitely need the desire and the ability to go that extra mile that is required for running the marathon of life even on your journey to financial freedom.

Determination therefore becomes a critical tool for one to follow through with life's decisions and determination as we have indicated earlier refers to willpower, strength of mind, resolve, fortitude, purposefulness, and resilience. All these, the prodigal son had, which propelled him to follow through with his decision to return to the father's house to better his financial lot in life.

5

Duty To Act On Your Decision

"Thinking is easy, acting is difficult, and to put one's thoughts into action is the most difficult thing in the world.
Johann Wolfgang Von Goethe

We have seen from the preceding two chapters that, making decisions to do something in life coupled with cultivating the spirit of determination to follow through with those decisions is very critical to success. Nonetheless, in this current chapter, we shall see that the above notwithstanding, success in any field of endeavour in life is contingent upon the actions taken in relation to the decisions we reach in life. We shall therefore be considering the duty we owe ourselves to act on our decisions to bring them to tangible and material fruition. Note that the chapter is not merely about how to act on a decision you have reached, but we say *"The Duty to Act on Your Decision"*. The term 'Duty' therefore makes the demand for action not voluntary, but obligatory and mandatory.

Duty is a contractual obligation to perform a task or an assignment. In the pursuit of financial freedom, one of the cardinal ingredients is the duty to act on our decisions.

Many dreams, visions, plans and aspirations of life though potentially very viable and powerful were never achieved because, they were never implemented. The action stage of any process is the most daunting, intimidating, challenging, overwhelming, disheartening, demoralizing and scary, to say the least.

Many people therefore never get past this

stage because it confronts the realities of life. This is where the successful and failures in life are determined. It is also the stage of progress in life where the boys are separated from the men and girls from the real women.

The journey of a thousand miles is accomplished one-step at a time, nevertheless; the first of these steps is the most critical of them all. Once you are able to take that all-important first step, the remaining steps become a routine that result in miles until you get to your destination. It is often not the full distance of the journey to success and financial freedom that scares or stops most of the people from embarking on the journey but rather the boldness to take the first step.

The prodigal son was not merely determined but he actually acted on his decision. Our reference scripture in Luke chapter 15 indicates that the prodigal son did indeed act on his decision to arise and go back to the father. In the verse 18 he indicated that he would arise and go to his father and we see him act on that word in the verse 20 where the scripture recorded that "**And he arose, and came to his father...?**

Luke 15:18-20
*18 **I will arise and go to my father**, and will say unto him, Father, I have sinned against heaven, and before thee,*
19 And am no more worthy to be called thy son: make me as one of thy hired servants.
*20 **And he arose, and came to his father**. But when he was yet a great way off, his father saw him, and had compassion, and ran, and fell on his neck, and kissed him.*

In life, any desire you cannot back with the right actions is a mere wish and wishes do not amount to anything tangible but fantasies. Actions are the success knobs that turn the door of desire open for you to obtain the tangible, material and physical equivalent of the intangible substances of desire.

Desire minus action equals imagination whereas desire plus action equals tangible, material and physical manifestations. Your dreams in life will remain intangible and imaginative junk until they provoke action in you. Little dreams backed by definite action will yield more tangible results than great and fascinating dreams that never see an action.

It is not how many dreams or expectations you have that makes the difference in your life, but rather the actions you are able to take on those dreams and expectation.

Psalm 1:1-3

Blessed is the man that walketh not in the counsel of the ungodly, nor standeth in the way of sinners, nor sitteth in the seat of the scornful. [2] But his delight is in the law of the Lord; and in his law doth he meditate day and night. [3] And he shall be like a tree planted by the rivers of water, that bringeth forth his fruit in his season; his leaf also shall not wither; **and**

whatsoever he doeth shall prosper.

The verse 3 of the above scriptural passage rightly hits the nail on the head. It is what that blessed man does that brings the financial prosperity; meaning that the prospering is in the doing of the positive things that attract financial prosperity rather than the mere abstinence from the negative tendencies that will not bring prosperity. The decision, not to walk in the counsel of the ungodly, nor stand in the way of sinners, nor sit in the seat of the scornful is good; nevertheless, it is what you do that shall prosper you.

Financial freedom requires definite actions on your part and you cannot substitute action for anything in the pursuit of financial freedom. You cannot talk your dreams into performance, neither can you wish them into being. Unless you take definite action toward achieving those dreams, you will only harvest the wind. Actions are definite, daily, routine activities directed at achieving set goals. They are actionable goals and objectives that one pursues passionately in order to attain his or her financial freedom.

Financial freedom does not just happen. You need to take action on your financial objectives and goals. If you need to save or invest toward attaining financial freedom, you will need to make a deliberate effort to save and invest. It will not happen, just because you made up your mind or resolved to save. You will need to go to your bank and place a standing order that a certain amount of money be moved into a savings or investment account every month.

There are many people with nice personal investment plans and decisions to start investing who have never been able to cultivate the habit of taking action on those plans and decisions simply because, they have not obligated themselves to the task or duty of taking action on their decisions. You do not need a prophet to tell you that such people will never attain financial freedom. You must walk your talk and act on your decisions in order to see tangible results in any field of endeavour in life, be it in your career or finances; because actions they say speak louder than words.

The actions we take on our decisions produce the tangible results. Decisions we make, are in themselves powerless until action is initiated on them. The process of manifestation has a formula that teaches that thoughts lead to feelings, feelings lead to actions, and actions lead to results.

Millions of people "think" about getting rich and thousands and thousands of people do affirmations, visualizations, and meditations for getting rich. You can meditate almost every day. Yet you will never sit there meditating or visualizing and have a bag of money drop on your head or into your opened arms.

Note also that you are not the only person who must take action in order to succeed in life, everyone has to. So don't see yourself as one of those really unfortunate ones who actually have to **do** something to be a success financially.

Affirmations, meditations, and visualizations are all wonderful tools, but as far as I can tell, none of them on its own is going to bring you real money in the real world. In the real world, you have to take real "action" to succeed. Why is action so critical?

Action is the "bridge" between the inner world and the outer world.

Action is so critical to financial freedom because, when you look again at the process of manifestation, you will notice that thoughts and feelings are part of the inner world whereas results are part of the outer world. That means action is the "bridge" between the inner world and the outer world.

Since we are creatures of habit, we need to practice acting in spite of fright, in spite of reservation, in spite of apprehension, in spite of uncertainty, in spite of inconvenience, in spite of discomfort, and even to practice acting when we are not in the disposition to act.

In the next few pages before we end the chapter, we want to consider some factors or boosters that can serve as triggers for action in the pursuit of financial dreams. We will end by looking at some other factors that serve as hindrances to action, which you will do well to avoid or surmount in your effort to embark on the journey to financial freedom.

Seven Triggers of Action for Financial Freedom

Actions are practical steps taken toward achieving set goals or objectives and can be triggered by several factors among which are the following: motivation, passion, time consciousness, purposefulness, knowledge, association and the right environment.

1. Your Motivation For Financial Freedom

What is your motivation for wanting to attain financial freedom or be financially independent? Is it so you could be your own boss or that you could have total freedom or control over your time and your pay cheque? Could it also be that you want to be able to quit your 9 to 5 routine that sometimes makes you work overtime and have tight work schedules and thus leaving you with no time for family and leisure?

Whatever your motivation may be for desiring financial freedom, you must understand that that motivation could become the trigger for action toward achieving your financial goals in life.

Motivation is the internal or external force that gives somebody a reason or incentive to do or want to do something. It is a feeling of enthusiasm, interest, or commitment that makes somebody want to do something, or something that causes such a feeling. If your motivation for financial freedom is strong enough, it becomes a trigger for action even in the face of the strongest inertia. If you really desire to take action on your decision to embark on the journey to financial freedom, then you must develop a strong motivation for financial freedom that can become the driving force to trigger actions toward achieving your financial goals. This you can achieve by setting your mind's eyes on the incentives and rewards of the financial freedom you will gain instead of the task involved in gaining the financial freedom.

2. Your Passion For Financial Freedom

Passion is an intense or overpowering emotion such as love, joy, hatred, or anger. It is the object of somebody's intense interest or enthusiasm, a strong liking or enthusiasm for a subject or activity. Passion is the catalyst for success.

The highest paid and most successful people in our society do what they love to do, as much of the time as they possibly can. You should continually be standing back, examining yourself objectively, and then practicing the habit of focusing on your special talents and abilities that generate your strongest passion.

Each person is born with the ability to do one or more things in an exceptional fashion. Just as you have multiple intelligences, you can have multiple abilities as well. The multiple abilities coupled with the multiple intelligences you have become the seat of passion in your life.

Just as you will only really be happy and successful when you find the kind of work that taps into the unique talents you have today, or which you can develop tomorrow. In the same way, your financial success largely depends on your passion to succeed financially. How passionate you are toward your desire and decision to become financially independent will be a driving force and a trigger of action toward your financial goal.

When determination fails, passion takes the driver's seat in the life of any visionary person. The intensity of your passion for financial freedom therefore would be a key indicator of your ability to take prompt actions and to seize opportunities to attain financial freedom in your personal life.

3. Your Time Consciousness

Time is the only universal resource with the fairest distribution *(time and chance hapeneth to them all)*. It is however, also the most perishable universal resource. Time is a non-renewable resource, which when lost can never be renewed or regained. Time cannot be stored in any retrievable form, you cannot preserve it in any form, and you cannot slow it down or make it to wait for any man. You can neither programme nor de-programme it to suit your preference, because *"Time and Tide wait for no man."*

Time consciousness simply means; having an understanding of the fact that our lives are lived within the confines of time and seasons and for that matter planning our lives to be fully utilised within the confines of the time available to us.

Realizing that life is short, helps us to use the little time we have more wisely and for eternal good and for that matter be inspired to take appropriate actions promptly to redeem the time.

According to *Eccles. 3:1* "To **everything there is a season,** and a **time to every purpose** *under the heaven:"*

Understanding the above scripture is critical to your consciousness with time.

You must understand that in life, everybody has his/her season and that every stage of our lives is like a season for a specific assignment - including our pursuit of financial freedom - and if you miss that season, you miss out on life. You must also understand that every purpose of God goes with a time frame and so we must do everything to stay in time with the purposes of God for our lives.

One of the ways to become effective with your time consciousness and thereby trigger actions in the pursuit of your desire and decision to attain financial freedom is to set goals for your financial life and pursue them. Goal setting is a powerful process for personal planning in any area of your life including your financial life.

The process of setting financial goals helps you choose where you want to go in life financially. By knowing precisely what you want to achieve financially, you know where you have to concentrate your efforts toward financial freedom. You will also quickly spot the distractions that would otherwise lure you from your course.

You will also be required to seize opportunities in your life as they present themselves. Do not wait for the convenient time, for there is no such time as convenient time.

Eccles. 11:4 (KJV)
He that observeth the wind shall not sow; and he that regardeth the clouds shall not reap.

Eccles. 11:4 (NLT)
If you wait for perfect conditions, you will never get anything done.

Waiting for perfect conditions will mean inactivity. This practical insight is especially applicable to your financial life. If you wait for the perfect time and investment opportunities, you will never begin. If you wait for a perfect job, you will never accept one. If you wait for the perfect market conditions or economic conditions, you will never start investing or building your future financial fortune. Take steps now to grow financially. Do not wait for conditions that may never exist.

Finally, you must be aware of time robbers in order to steer clear off their destructive effect so that your effort to become time conscious can serve as a trigger to induce action toward achieving your financial goals promptly.

These time robbers include procrastination indecision, socializing, interruptions, unclear personal goals and poor planning among many others.

> *"A wise person does at once, what a fool does at last. Both do the same thing; only at different times."*
>
> *Baltasar Gracian),*

4. Your Purpose and Vision for Financial Freedom

If you know that you have a great destiny in life, you will not allow the trivialities of life to derail you from achieving that destiny. This is the reason why it is imperative to discover your purpose for being in life very early so that you will know how to live your life and not miss your eternal destiny.

We can define purpose as the reason for which something exists. It answers the question "**WHY?**" Why am I here? Why do I want to attain financial freedom? Why did I establish that company? Why does that business exist?

There are many people alive today who should have been entrepreneurs with great businesses and companies to their names. There are people who should be providing employment opportunities for many hundreds or thousands of folks out there, but who have themselves ended up as employees of other entrepreneurs. There are people out there who should be running educational institutions of great renown but who have ended up becoming classroom teachers in other public or private educational institutions. This is because they failed to discover their real purpose for being.

When you do not know your purpose for being, you will only end up becoming a part of another man's purpose.

If you want to have a vision for your financial future, you must know the purpose of for your financial life. Your purpose or assignment in life gives birth to your vision. Your vision is the mental picture of what you want to achieve or become in future. Without vision, leadership accomplishes nothing. Without a vision the people perish, they wander aimlessly, the people dwell carelessly. Therefore, without financial vision, you will possibly become reckless and irresponsible in dealing with your finances.

Proverbs 29:18
Where there is no vision, the people perish:

but he that keepeth the law, happy is he.

In life, you cannot go beyond how far you can dream to go. You cannot go to any destination you cannot picture in your mind's eyes. Anything you cannot perceive or conceive in life, you cannot achieve.

Vision therefore becomes the foundational requirement for every attainment in life, including financial empowerment. Your altitude in life determines your horizon (perspective, sphere, scope) and your horizon sets the seal to your reach in life.

Genesis 13:14-15
And the Lord said unto Abram, after that Lot was separated from him, **Lift up now thine eyes, and look from the place where thou art** *northward, and southward, and eastward, and westward: [15] For* **all the land which thou seest, to thee will I give it, and to thy seed for ever.**

A vision is a mental picture of a desired future state. It is the picture of a desired destination one dreams of and works towards getting to.

From a personal financial point of view, a vision may therefore be said to be a mental picture of an expected future financial destination or position an individual desires to attain in order to attain financial freedom.

Jeremiah 1:11-12 (KJV)

Moreover the word of the Lord came unto me, saying, ***Jeremiah, what seest thou?*** *And* ***I said, I see a rod of an almond tree****. [12] Then said the Lord unto me,* ***Thou hast well seen****: for I will hasten my word to perform it.*

Amos 7:7-8 (KJV)

Thus he shewed me: and, behold, the Lord stood upon a wall made by a plumbline, with a plumbline in his hand. [8] And ***the Lord said*** *unto me, Amos, what seest thou? And I said, A plumbline.* Then said the Lord, Behold, I will set a plumbline in the midst of my people Israel: I will not again pass by them any more:

Until you can see it with your mind's eyes, your mind cannot conceive it and the hands cannot pursue it.

The Role of Vision in Attaining Financial Freedom

i. Why do you want to be financially free?
Vision determines the purpose of the financial empowerment one desires.

ii. How much of wealth do you want to acquire?
Vision helps fix in your mind the exact amount of money or financial empowerment you desire to achieve.

iii. How do you intend to attain the financial freedom you so desire.

Vision enables you to determine what exactly you want to give in exchange for the money or financial empowerment you desire. **"There Is Nothing Like Something for Nothing"**

iv. At what time do you want to reach your financial dream?

Vision enables you to fix a definite date when you intend to possess the money you desire.

v. What steps do you intend to follow in the pursuit of your financial dream?

Vision enables you to create a definite plan for carrying out your desire for your financial empowerment.

If you discover your financial purpose in life and are able to develop a strong attainable vision for your financial freedom, it will trigger action in your personal financial pursuits

5. Your Knowledge in Financial Empowerment

Knowledge and skill are paramount to

attaining financial freedom of any appreciable quantum. Therefore, to achieve any level of financial freedom you have never achieved before, you will have to develop and master one or more skills that you have never had before that can boost your earning capability and motivate you to take actions on you financial freedom goals.

A skill is the same as a habit of performance, and like habits, you can learn all skills you will ever need in life. You can learn any skill you need to learn to achieve any goal that you can set for yourself. If anyone else around you has acquired a key knowledge or developed a key skill that has enabled him or her to be more successful, that is proof in itself that you too can acquire this knowledge and learn this skill. It is simply a matter of practice and repetition.

The Law of Self-Development requires that you make a list of the key skills and the knowledge set that is essential for success in your field. There are usually only about 5-7 skills, or key result areas, that determine most of the success that one achieves in any field of endeavour. Your first job is to identify these key skills and write them down.

You have achieved the current level of success in your field because of your talent and ability in certain key areas. Nevertheless, at the same time, you have failed to move forward because of your weaknesses in other areas. The rule is that your weakest key skill determines the height of your results, and your earning power. In other words, you could be excellent at six out of seven key result areas, but your weakness in the seventh area will determine your overall results and rewards in that job or field.

You therefore ask yourself this question, "What one skill, if I developed and did it consistently in an excellent fashion, would have the greatest positive impact on my career and financial ambition?"

You must develop the habit of continually identifying and working on your weakest key skill. Bringing up your ability in this one area will usually have a greater and immediate impact on your results than anything else you can do and that has the potential to trigger action in your pursuit of financial freedom.

Another key habit for self-development is to become growth oriented. Growth orientation requires that you develop the habit of continuous learning, the habit of continuous personal and professional development.

Just as you exercise physically on a regular basis to remain fit and healthy, you must exercise mentally on a daily basis to become better and better in your chosen field.

The Law of Cause and Effect says that if you do what other successful people do, you will eventually get the same results other successful people get. This is not a wish or theory. It is a universal law. The law itself is neutral and therefore works for everybody, everywhere.

6. Your Association with Experts

The power of right association can influence your decision to pursue any wealth plan and induce action toward your decision to embark on the journey to financial freedom. One key way to achieve this is to rub minds with and learn from the experts through the habit of attending every seminar and course you possibly can.

Do not make the mistake of waiting for courses and seminars to come to you, or waiting for your company to organize and pay for additional training. You are completely responsible for your own life, which includes your own personal financial and professional development. No one cares as much about your financial future and your career as you do. No one cares about your ability to increase your income and move into the top bracket of your field as much as you do. You are fully responsible for that.

You must understand also that something remarkable takes place in an adult learning environment, which is completely different from attending a required course in college or university. The types of people who attend adult seminars are of a much higher calibre than you meet in your day-to-day life. They are more positive; more highly motivated, have bigger and better goals, and are more determined to succeed.

When you spend several hours in their company, it has a subtle but powerful subconscious effect on you. You actually become a better and more focused person by the very act of associating with other successful people in an adult learning situation or seminar, which has the ability to stimulate you for action toward pursuing and achieving your financial empowerment goals.

Make it a habit to seek out and attend at least four seminar programmes per year in your field. If your organization has annual or national conventions, be sure to attend. Eagerly seek out and sit in on the most important talks and lectures at each of these workshops or annual meetings. Sometimes, one good idea from an expert in your field can transform your entire career and financial landscape and trigger action toward achieving financial freedom.

7. Your Environment

Your environment consists of the natural surroundings in which you live or exist considered in relation to their physical characteristics or weather conditions and the people who live in them. Someone's environment is all the circumstances, people, things, and events around them that influence their lives.

i. Internal environment

The internal environment of a person refers

to the mental and emotional dispositions of the individual that determine how that individual responds to internal stimuli. It consists of the inborn traits, thought processes, behavioural patterns, attitudes, feelings, etc. of the person.

ii. External environment

The external environment on the other hand involves all the things outside the individual's life such as all the circumstances, people, things, and events around them that influence their lives.

The combined force of these two environmental influences produces the personality of the individual. The question however, is whether personality really matters in becoming successful financially? Recent studies say yes, successful people share a number of common personality traits, and these traits are the predominant indicators of their success outweighing education, family ties, skills and experience. Moreover, people who choose business ventures, careers, investment tools and personal financial plans that are in harmony with their true personalities tend to experience the greatest level of financial success and fulfilment.

Every personality type and therefore, every person has the potential to achieve financial success. You just need to determine the right opportunity. Self-awareness guides us in understanding what we will need to bridge the gap between who we are and what the opportunity requires.

By the Law of Correspondence, your outer world will always be a reflection of your inner world. If you therefore, want to change something in your outer world, or achieve a goal that you have never achieved in the past, you are going to have to change your inner world in some way.

When there is positive correspondence between your inner world and your outer world, then your inner dispositions can positively influence your outer decision and thereby becoming a trigger for action toward your financial decisions.

Six Forces that Act as Hindrances to Action toward Financial Freedom

1. Inertia to Act

Inertia is the inability or unwillingness to move or act.

Prov. 26:14, 15
14 As the door turns upon its hinges, so does the lazy man turn upon his bed. 15 The lazy man hides his hand in his bosom; it grieves him to bring it again to his mouth.

Many people are unable or unwilling to act on their financial objectives and decisions because of the inconvenience they anticipate. Nothing worthwhile in life is convenient doing. Many things in life will inconvenience you but that notwithstanding, you must still practice acting on your financial objectives. Seeking convenient opportunities, convenient methods, convenient times and convenient places before we act in life is therefore the first root cause of inertia in many lives.

Now that we have addressed convenience as the first root cause of inertia, we shall look at the next root cause of inertia, which is "comfort". Why is acting in spite of discomfort so important? Because, the place called "comfortable" is where you currently are now, which is causing the inertia you are suffering from right now. If you want to move to a new level in your financial life, you must break through your comfort zone and practice doing things that are not comfortable.

The secret to great destinies is the forfeiture of the comfort of what we are today for what we could become which may be uncomfortable.

Many great financial destinies have been stifled for fear of moving out of the comfort zone to try something challenging that may cause some discomfort. Being comfortable may make you feel warm and secure, but it does not allow you to grow. To grow as a person you have to expand beyond your comfort zone. The only time you can actually grow is when you are *outside* your comfort zone.

Isa. 54:2-4
*2 **Make the place of your tent larger**, and let them **stretch out the curtains of your dwellings**. Do not spare, **lengthen your cords** and **strengthen your stakes**;*
*3 for **you shall break out on the right hand and on the left**. And your seed shall inherit the nations, and people will inhabit ruined cities.*
4 Do not fear; for you shall not be ashamed, nor shall you blush; for you shall not be put to shame; for you shall forget the shame of your youth, and shall not remember the reproach of your widowhood any more.

The final root cause of inertia is the feeling

of not being in the mood to act. You do not need to feel or be in the mood to act before you act on the goals and decisions you make in life. You just need to act because you must act.

Many people want to wait until they get that tickling effect before they act. There is no such thing as the right feeling or right mood for acting on your financial decisions. Money does not have emotions or moods, so why do you want to wait until you have emotions or are in the mood before you take actions to acquire the money you need for your financial freedom?

2. Procrastination

Bernard Meltzer very well reflects the essence of procrastination in this quote:

"Hard work is often the easy work you did not do at the proper time."

Briefly, you procrastinate when you put off things that you should be focusing on right now, usually in favour of doing something that is more enjoyable or that you are more comfortable doing.

Sometimes this happens when someone does not understand the difference between urgency and importance. We all have the same amount of time in every day and procrastinators spend this time fully, but do not invest it wisely. Instead, they focus so much on urgent issues that they have little or no time left for the important tasks, despite the unpleasant outcomes this may bring about.

Among the typical reasons why people procrastinate are: waiting for the right mood and waiting for the right time. There can never be the perfect mood or perfect time to take charge of your financial destiny. Seize the opportunities as they present themselves and do not wait for a perfect time, which will never come.

3. Fear

Prov. 26:13
The lazy one says, There is a lion in the way; a lion is in the streets.

So if action is so important, what prevents us from taking the actions we know we need to take toward financial freedom? It is Fear of course!

Fear, doubt, and worry are among the greatest obstacles or hindrances, not only to financial success, but to happiness as well. Therefore, one of the biggest differences between rich people and poor people is that rich people are willing to act in spite of fear. Poor people let fear stop them.

Susan Jeffers even wrote a fantastic book about this, entitled *Feel the Fear and Do It Anyway*. The biggest mistake most people make is waiting for the feeling of fear to subside or disappear before they are willing to act.

These people usually wait forever.

Do not try to kill the monster called fear but at least you can domesticate it. You do not need to get rid of the monster as well, and you certainly do not need to run away from the monster called fear. What we are saying for sure is to "tame" or domesticate the monster called fear.

It is not necessary to try to get rid of fear in order to succeed. Rich people act in spite of fear. Poor people let fear stop them.

It is imperative to realize that it is not necessary to try to get rid of fear in order to succeed. Rich and successful people have fear, rich and successful people have doubts, rich and successful people have worries. They just do not let these feelings stop them. Unsuccessful people have fears, doubts, and worries, then let those feelings stop them.

4. Uncertainty

Whenever you make a financial or investment decision, there is some uncertainty about the outcome. **Uncertainty** means not knowing exactly what will happen in the future. There is uncertainty in almost everything we do regarding our financial lives, because no one knows precisely what changes will occur in such things as tax laws, consumer demand, the economy, or interest rates.

Though the terms "risk" and "uncertainty" are often used to mean the same thing, there is a distinction between them. Uncertainty is not knowing what's going to happen. **Risk** is how we characterize *how much* uncertainty exists: The greater the uncertainty, the greater the risk and greater the returns on the investment. The greater the uncertainty, the greater the disincentive of the risk averse individual to want invest and therefore the stronger the unwillingness to take action on decisions that lead to financial freedom.

5. Opportunity Cost

Opportunity cost is the cost of a commercial or investment decision regarded as the value of the alternative that is forgone. Anytime you make a decision to invest your money, what you are actually doing is postponing the gratification that you could derive from that money today.

Investing is the act of committing money or capital to an endeavour with the expectation of obtaining an additional income or profit. When you decide to put aside any money and allow it to work for you until it brings the desired profit on a future date, you have in effect forfeited or at the same time sacrificed every other thing you could possibly use that money for today. For example, if instead of buying a new flat screen LCD television set, I choose rather to invest the money in to Treasury bill for one year, then my opportunity cost of investing in the T-bill becomes the LCD Television I have to sacrifice in order to free that money for investment.

Opportunity cost of investing is therefore the determination of what exactly you want to give in exchange for the money or financial empowerment you desire because, *"there is nothing like something for nothing"*. This therefore becomes the hindrance to many people's ability to take prompt action on their decision to invest for financial freedom because; they are either unwilling or unready to delay the gratifications of today for tomorrow. What the actions to invest will cost is what keeps many thousands from attaining financial freedom.

6. Past Experience

We are conditioned by specific incidents and experiences we have had in the past with money and that affects the way we act today in relation to money. What did you experience when you were young around money, wealth, and rich people? These experiences are extremely important because they shape the beliefs – or rather, the illusions –you now live by.

So what is your experience? Where are you coming from? Were you always successful? Like many other people today, you supposedly had a lot of "potential" but had little to show for it. May be you read all the books you knew of and could read, listened to all the tapes and went to all the seminars.

You really, really, really wanted to be successful. Though you did not know whether it was for the money, the freedom, the sense of achievement, or just to prove you were good enough in your parents' eyes. All the same, you were almost obsessed with becoming a "success." During your twenties, you started several different businesses, each with the dream of making your fortune, but your results went from dismal to worse.

You probably worked your butt off but kept coming up short because you had heard of this thing called profit, you just never saw any of it. You kept thinking, "if you just could get into the right business, get on the right horse, you will make it," but you were wrong.

Nothing was working –at least for you and may be you wondered how others were succeeding in the exact same business you were in and you were still broke? Then you tend to examine your true beliefs and saw that even though you said you really wanted to be rich, you had some deep-rooted worries about it. Mostly, you were afraid. Afraid that you might fail, or worse, succeed and then somehow lose it all. Your "story" that you had all this "potential", what if you found out you did not have what it took and you were destined to a life of struggle.

6

Diligence To The Actions Of Your Decision

Never ever, give up and keep going until you reach your dreams. Trust the idea towards wealth. Believe in the fact that hard work pays because it will compensate you soon. It is about the burning desire to win the financial battle. We are born champions.

Proverbs 21:5
The thoughts of the diligent tend only to plenteousness; but of every one that is hasty only to want.

The counsels, reckonings, and calculations

of the diligent increase his abundance; but he who is hasty, impatient, and restless in his pursuit of gain will not succeed.

Proverbs 10:4
He becometh poor that dealeth with a slack hand: but the hand of the diligent maketh rich.

Diligence is a persistent and hard-working effort in doing something. It also means assiduousness, persistence, industriousness, tirelessness, and hardworking. Most of the actions you will take in life will require diligence to succeed and to be excellent.

Proverbs 12:27
The slothful man roasteth not that which he took in hunting: but the substance of a diligent man is precious.

If you want to create wealth or any other kind of success, you have to be a fighter who will never give up in the face of any challenge.

You have to be willing to do whatever it takes. You have to 'train' yourself not to be stoppable by anything.

Getting rich is not always convenient. Getting rich is not always easy. In fact, getting rich can be damn hard. If you are willing to do only what is easy, life will always be hard for you. However, if you are willing to do what is hard then life will be easy for you. Rich people don't base their actions on what is easy and convenient; that way of living is reserved for the poor and most of the middle class.

If you are willing to do only easy things in life, life will be hard for you. Nevertheless, if you are willing to do what is hard then life will be easy for you.

Proverbs 13:4
*The soul of the sluggard desireth, and hath nothing: but **the soul of the diligent shall be made fat**.*

Proverbs 22:29

Seest thou a man diligent in his business? he shall stand before kings; he shall not stand before mean men.

If you are not achieving the wealth you say you desire, there is a good chance it is because, you are not willing to do what it takes to create it.

There are actually three levels of the so-called wanting to be financially free. The first level is **"I *want* to be rich."** That is another way of saying, "I'll take it if it falls in my laps." Wanting alone is useless. Have you noticed that wanting does not necessarily lead to "having"?

You ought to understand that wanting without having, leads to more wanting. Wealth however, does not come from merely wanting it. How do you know this is true? With a simple reality check, you will find out that there are millions of people world over that *want* to be rich, yet relatively few people are rich. This is so because wants are either mere wishful desires or longings but nothing, and you cannot wish yourself into becoming a millionaire. It requires time, resources, effort, hard work and diligence.

The second level of wanting is "**I *choose* to be rich.**" This entails deciding to become rich. Choosing is a much stronger energy and goes hand in hand with being responsible for creating your reality. The word *decision* comes from the Latin word *decidere,* which means, ***"to kill off any other alternatives."*** Choosing is better but still not best.

The third level of wanting is "**I *commit* to being rich.**" The definition of the word *commit* is ***"to devote oneself unreservedly."*** This means holding absolutely nothing back but giving hundred percent of everything you have got to achieving wealth. It means being willing to do whatever it takes and for as long as it takes. No excuses, no ifs, no buts, no may bes –and failure is not an option. "I will be rich or I will die trying." It is as simple as that.

Many a people would never truly be willing to commit themselves, resources or time to becoming rich. If you should ask the average person walking about in life a simple question like, "Would you bet your life that in the next so and so years you will be wealthy?" most would say, "No way!" That is the difference between rich people and poor people. It is precisely because, people are not ready to commit themselves to being rich that is why they are not rich and most likely never will be rich.

You might say a thing like this, "I work my butt off, trying real hard. Of course I'm committed to being rich." Trying you may, but the truth is that your trying means little. The definition of *commitment* is to devote oneself unreservedly. The key word is "unreservedly", which means you are putting everything, and I mean everything you have into it. You will meet most of the people you know who are not financially successful and yet they have limits to how much they are willing to do, how much they are willing to risk, and how much they are willing to sacrifice.

Although you may think, you are willing to do whatever it takes to become financially sound, upon deeper reflection you will always find out that you have many conditions around what you are willing to do and not do to succeed financially.

What I am about to tell you is not pleasant or exciting to tell you, but the truth is, getting rich is not a stroll in the park, and anyone who tells you it is, either knows a lot more than those who think so and have made their millions that way or the person is just a little out of integrity or is naive.

From experience, getting rich takes focus, courage, knowledge, expertise, hundred percent of your effort, a never-give-up attitude, and of course a rich mind-set. You also have to believe in your heart of hearts that you can create wealth and that you absolutely deserve it. Again, what this means is that, if you are not fully, totally, and truly committed to creating wealth, chances are you will not.

If you are not fully, totally, and truly committed to creating wealth, chances are you will not.

Are you willing to work sixteen hours or more a day? Many rich people are. Are you willing to work seven days a week and give up most of your weekends? Most of the rich people are. Are you willing to sacrifice seeing your family, your friends, and give up your leisure, recreations and hobbies? Rich people are. Are you willing to risk all your time, energy, and start-up capital with no guarantee of returns? Rich people are.

For a time, hopefully a short time but most

often for a long haul of time, rich people are ready and willing to do all of the above. Are you? Until you are too, you have no business with what we have been discussing so far. So make up your mind right now before you drop this book.

Maybe you will be lucky such that you will not have to work long or hard or sacrifice anything. You can wish for that, but the bitter truth is that you sure cannot count on it. Again, rich people are committed enough to do whatever it takes.

It is interesting to note, however, that once you do commit yourself to give up anything; from family, your friends, your leisure, recreations and hobbies and you are willing to risk all your time, energy, and start-up capital, the universe will stoop to support you. In other words, the universe will assist you, guide you, support you, and even create miracles for you. Nevertheless, you first need to commit yourself.

Mark 10:28-30

*28 Peter began to say unto him, Lo, **we have left all, and have followed thee.***

*29 Jesus said, Verily I say unto you, **There is no man that hath left house, or brethren, or sisters, or mother, or father, or children, or lands, for my sake, and for the gospel's sake,***

*30 **but he shall receive a hundredfold now in this time, houses, and brethren, and sisters, and mothers, and children, and lands, with persecutions**; and in the world to come eternal life.*

Proverbs 27:23-27

23 Be thou diligent to know the state of thy flocks, and look well to thy herds.

24 For riches are not forever: and doth the crown endure to every generation?

25 The hay appeareth, and the tender grass sheweth itself, and herbs of the mountains are gathered.

26 The lambs are for thy clothing, and the

goats are the price of the field.

27 And thou shalt have goats' milk enough for thy food, for the food of thy household, and for the maintenance for thy maidens.

www.ingramcontent.com/pod-product-compliance
Lightning Source LLC
Chambersburg PA
CBHW051714170526
45167CB00002B/651